Neptune Park

Also by Daniel Tiffany

Theory and Criticism

Radio Corpse: Imagism and the Cryptaesthetic of Ezra Pound
Harvard University Press, 1995

Toy Medium: Materialism and Modern Lyric
University of California Press, 2000

Infidel Poetics: Riddles, Nightlife, Substance
University of Chicago Press, 2009

In the Poisonous Candy Factory
Capsule Editions (London, UK), 2013

My Silver Planet: A Secret History of Poetry and Kitsch
Johns Hopkins University Press, 2013

Poetry

Puppet Wardrobe
Parlor Press, 2006

Privado
Action Books, 2010

The Dandelion Clock
Tinfish Press, 2010

Brick Radio
Oystercatcher Press (Norfolk, UK), 2013

Neptune Park

daniel tiffany

OMNIDAWN PUBLISHING
RICHMOND, CALIFORNIA
2013

Cover photograph © John Divola
From *Vandalism Series, 74V08, 1974*

Book interior design by Cassandra Smith

Offset printed in the United States
by Edwards Brothers Malloy, Ann Arbor, Michigan
on Glatfelter Natures Natural 55# Recycled 30% PCW
Acid Free Archival Quality FSC Certified Paper

Cataloguing-in-Publication Data is available from the Library of Congress

Published by Omnidawn Publishing, Richmond, California
www.omnidawn.com   (510) 237-5472   (800) 792-4957
10 9 8 7 6 5 4 3 2 1
ISBN: 978-1-890650-86-5

This book is for
MOLLY BENDALL
of Richmond,
Virginia

CONTENTS

I shrink from giving too many of the names, shunning the unpleasant task of writing them down — unless it comports with the pleasure of someone to hear "Pleutaurans," "Bardyetans," "Allotrigans," and other names still less pleasing and of less significance than these.

Strabo, *Geography*

CORRECTION

HE'S JUST A DOLLAR SIGN TO ME

You ask what I look like.
Crows are flying home from school,
the wind is blowing hard.

Dear little revelers
come hopping along.
Please play my favorite nocturne!

Beautiful lobbies
will be ghosting millionaire brides,
shortly to be replaced

by insects, dolls, and
cake, cake and cutty,
my Cutlass Supreme.

Or who can stay
the bottles of heaven?
Blank and popped

or painted phoenix
yellow, the mind swallows the bait,
any rumor of pilgrims

crushed at the gate.
The blueness of a wound
cleans away rancor.

When someone goes,
someone remains.
Even out of the thorns

the robber swallows up
my ration, swallows hard
on the hook.

FRONTING

Mostly the creeps turn their heads
so as to not see us.

A repeated phrase glitters on the threshold.
My boyfriends drink out of a dark

green puddle. *What is Man
that thou should magnify him?*

Then, too, then, too, then, too,
the Bardot girls listen for strangers

back home. Lucky that
grimy curtain doesn't do much

to hide the bed.
Pepper three-way

now your poppy-
bower syndrome, not all there

to feel the pranks my boyfriends
have in store for me.

FIREFLIES FOR SALE

Smoky, smoky tongue,
my beach-plum preserve—

where do they go?

You won't find a tearoom
in Spain or France;

it don't come in jars
in Spain or France.

*For that which is to be
hath already been.*

I'm writing an ode
to the nail parlor girls

and the doxy fumes.
Her soul is so hooked.

I saw two sparrows run a race,
I saw two horses making lace.

She won't think
it's nothing strange.

A dream comes through
—an alibi for sale—

through honeycomb
the sting of business.

Her face is covered,
her back is bare.

Something tapping my neck—

"an edict of Charlemagne"
I think she said.

BIRDNEST BOUND

It's easy to draw
a bread and buttermilk line
through Finland.

She fell and left her life
among the stars.
Alice never could be found.

Just as
the mistle-
toe in dead winter

grows a fresh leaf,
its own and not
its host's.

All the mob
comes pouring
to shore.

Birdnest bound,
birdnest builded
on the ground.

Alice never could be found,
a tin of kissing comfits in her pocket.
What,

any medium
can be stiffened
with pearl,

with her *ain't-gonna-play-*
no-secret-no-more look
back, I say.

Still got that throwing-away burning away.

The mouth she asks
this with:
flint, flour, dent, pop.

Something for the horse.

NEPTUNE FIX

Take us the foxes
the little foxes
who spoil the vines,
take it to my used-to-be.

O take me to the waterfront
where the water runs cold.

Then the world wants to know
what this all about.

Neither say thou
before the angel
ROYAL RIDING.
Never ever.

(And just for the record
the two long hours
it took to set the trap
seemed not long to him at all.)

The human torch is the main attraction.

And the visor?
A simple way to earn a few style points.

People run all over town.

Wilt thou set thine eyes
upon that which is not?

Nonstop.

Even when I remember
I am afraid.

The "bears" stopped at my house first,
done me all the harm they could.

Judging
by the amount of lipstick

I found, I would say
between 6 and 8 times.

She's still sleeping.

Put some of that in there.

TOUCHING TOPICS

Every night about four
or it might be half past
friends dig through the houses
they mark for themselves.

Fling down the nests
and the gall will be done
felling an oak
to set up a strawberry.

No more than
the world can take.

You look like somebody
just turned you loose.

A flying enemy makes a silver bridge
doing a little old something else.
That's the way the bare-
footed soul does.

As round as an apple
  as deep as a pail
it never cries out
  till it's caught by the tail.

Crying when it does
without, now learn to lose.
Not Keats in a letter
drafting children's midnight junkets.

I chose the walnut.

Whose fruiting body,
like a ball of twine
or the untidy turban,
is known to me.

A THEORY OF SUDDEN AND ASSISTED MUTATIONS

go back silhouette
look up
the strange words

between nobodies

your catch
such as it is
guessable for its switcheroo

had
everything I had
split the air

PULCHRITUDE

The birdless place
the Greeks named it.

Insufflation of you know what.

Followed quickly by some drone,
some doctor, now that you mention it,

bearing the proverbial cup
on a silver filigree stem.

I'll try a drop of that.

The hoarse divinities would parade
before the inventor of butterfly wings.

No subtext here,
people are naked.

Bartering with the guileless do I
even want to know?

Three little ghostesses
Sitting on postesses
Eating buttered toastesses
Greasing their fistesses
Up to their wristesses.

And mirth,
what does it do?

Crying I asked the spider did she
want her ashes hauled?

I asked my captain for the time of day.

"The unseen Titian,"
I think she said.

Il Tiziano mai visto.

And something else,
old friend:

try looking away.
You know the drill.

Try not helping.

Ah, a forest of somethings!
—that kind of thing.

And try to stop calling it *it*.

THE CONCEPT OF THE GENERAL STRIKE

To the south, to the south:
outlines of people running for cover, orchards

aflame and conjurings in green ink.
The songs pursue her.

Black water climbing
through windows and doors,

five feet from the ground,
five feet from the—

I mean ground.
And they are strange admirers of one another.

Faces scribbled with light
halfway through Seneca.

"I don't know what else to do."
Fast moving clouds.

Penny, as in pennyroyal, as in
tea for luckless girls.

Who's that marching up the road?

Mad white parasol
—in the sweet version.

And my lock was stolen.

INDUSTRY

ICING A GREAT CAKE ANOTHER WAY

Time is money.

And geese lower their heads
to pass under a bridge

no matter how high
the arch may be.

We're making bets
on your personal life.

Let's get cracking.

Primitive methods
candy up the squat

we call home.
What else?

It was raining.
There were motorcycles

spilled on the ground.
Take fast hold of instruction.

Because the world could be
ours, closer,

and smaller in the dark.
A maiden hurled a wheel

bristling with hearts and daggers.
We turned around

to look: no one.
The club went up in flames.

HOW MANY DAYS CAN YOU LIVE ON VICODIN AND FROSTY?

Poor thing, she holds him on her lap,
the godless hidden god,

causing the lips
of those that sleep to speak.

Cold shadow of the white
acanthus in its tiptoe dance.

Buy the truth
and sell it not.

A lion is in the streets,
there is a lion in the way.

My niece, the little siren,
taught her the slang:

mad married fiancée.

Dido has a quiver,
she wears a spotted lynx

skin and a belt.
My undefiled is not herself

tonight, but one thing's forever:
I just saw the video explaining

the neighborhood applause,
a book of anthems where sirens

plunge into the gold of the initials
at that karaoke party for her

boyfriend. We cooked up
all the goodies and fauns

came through the windows.
That's her thing.

"I like this path to darkness,"
she keeps saying.

Whatever party fame is doing to her
chances for a quick trial. You

can reach over and touch her hair.

By morning you'd know
if she was going to be back or not.

SILVER HAVOC

The sanctuary, properly speaking,
lies to the east of the reception room,

a pale of angel-coal on the doorstep.
The place is dark and in ruins.

Though she understands
she will not answer.

The grass winks
and blinks with fireflies.

Tiddle liddle lightum,
  pitch and tar;
Tiddle liddle lightum,
  what's that for?

Owing. The onset.

Better go somewheres else.

To be touched
they let themselves be tanked.

It held back.

They perish forever
without even telling me!

And if she walks with impunity
it is because, as usual,

she has placed her somatic vehicles
between parentheses.

Well, yes and no.

Dido is a perfectly fine name
but what does she know about boys?

Or cuff links.
Eyelid of the morning,

flakes of her flesh.
Nether millstone.

NOTHING BUT HALCYON AND BE REMISS

You look up at me and ask
if it's your turn to sing.
Racetracks and riddles

bring out the rogue
element, last time knocking
ever at my door.

Bo Peeper
Nose Dreeper
Chin Chopper.

White Lopper
Red Rag
and Little Gap.

This late-romantic region
where the borders are clocked
from dusk to dusk.

Withers being
wing to a chestnut.
Troth unmade,

as it usually is.

Am I a sea
that thou setteth
watch over me?

Spooked.
Lifer.
Fem-Agress.

Front cowl
on perch,
just like original.

Some begs
the jelly of that
teasing nell of mine.

And today is my actual birthday.

Blue, pink, and orange
silks. Oh keep me close
until thy wrath is done.

DUE DILIGENCE

His fingers have twelve years of piano
behind them.

From what rustic and debauched minds
do you inherit

such a pitiful neighing of diamonds?
Hence the name.

My sister threw a lit
candle at me for I had lingered

a moment too long.
All hypothetical of course.

Why mention ships
burned by the shore at Trestles?

Walk the streets all walk
the streets all night.

O the racetrack is a dusty place
and the cuckoo is a flying bird,
he hollers when he flies.

Pretty sure that corona
girl Dido gave me something
last night.

NEPTUNE SOCIETY

minted
like bambi
with brown bangs and ready-to-wears

serve to the one
she may will
I can tell my match

LIGHTNING AND FUR

'Tis pity thou art not
a bit more tongue-tied.

Here comes a candle
to light you to bed.

The sky comes down and howls
from stories of wolves

echo through the night.
I might start shimmering—

don't let nobody in.
The girl in the lane

who can't speak plain
cries *gobble gobble gobble*.

And when I use the word "serial"
I mean I've stolen a hat

from every guy who's followed me home unless
the last one, maybe.

I mean Colorado Blackie has a black rind,
I mean the oink in the moo.

I am referring of course
to the epigrammatic turn

this conversation is taking.
I don't need no made-up panic.

When the stormy kids we call
stars rise thick as hail,

I sometimes ask a question
then answer it myself.

It is surprising, I admit, to have to reason
with oneself in prison in order to be sad.

And when I say "complete whore"
I mean the kid leather

apron encircling his waist, the patch
of high birth upon his cap.

Mock epic.

I think I just scared a bird with my dick.

DEWSEAVILE

So much trouble
floating in the air.

Not an owl now, scratchy
bourbon *who-who*.

Her name trailing after that
plantation in that book.

Burnt and
about as easy to find.

I've got a new way of spelling
sweet old Dusieville.

Soaking goose liver in honey
and milk makes it larger.

Then you scare me with dreams
so that my soul chooses

strangling, like a drifter likes
the shadow, the gate.

I know I got some friends.

I know I got some friends don't
mess by the ditch at night.

HAVEN

A LIST OF TRANSNEPTUNIAN OBJECTS

But for netting and a scab
and for the bright spot
the molecules revert
to ships and plants.

So much so that fish
may be dried
and fitted with wicks.
A grass may cross the sea.

Still, one is not quite
a stranger to fountains,
to facing what sailors everywhere call
a water ghost,

the very wick of the stowaway kind.

Look, if I had wings
I could lie right here
flying past scenes of the apple,
scenes of the bucket,

over the ropes of all the wells.

FINGER AND THUMB

You could say she bottle-fed me
Jameson like I was a baby chimp

on one of those nature specials.
They have nice Easters over there.

She rigs the sport of Lady Lord
Macbeth, a little Goth

dragging along her clutter.
The law of the burnt offering.

Her hand on the head of the burnt offering.
Finger and thumb.

I tried on the queen's
dresses one by one.

It's a long old lane
and it's got no end.

It's a long old lane.

The sheep are gone
to the silver wood

and the nights are gone
to her majesty's son

all over my junk.
As I have heard

a reptile brag.

NUMBER FOUR STARING HIM IN THE FACE

It even has a spare fishing rod
and apparently grows a piece of bait
if it is brought into use.

So I spent the first 19 minutes
spinning around and one minute
licking the wall.

Never to have read
Voltaire and Rousseau.

Visible only by the darkest
green of their shadows.

You can't make anyone do anything.

Argon turns into chlorine,
xenon into fluorine.

And there's the devil behind
the glass making clothes for fishies,

everybody watching.
Said to traffick

in the silkworm of the sea,
capable of being woven into a golden fabric

from which gloves and
underthings used to be made.

Let others bow down
upon her.

She dresses "for the ball"
no matter what,

your sister, a mirror
with all the upgrades.

Zero reset.
Double tourbillon.

Monster
flyback.

German silver—
silver everything.

One of the coolest ways on the planet
to walk a big Mercedes.

And it's totally PRIVATE,
a girls-only evening.

MY SUPPLY OF THINGS TO TELL YOU

return to twentieth century
false transcription by
cat caption
looks like here of late

dance down unfinished
stairs close the
hatchway, sorry, lantern
blinded by foliage

HALF THE WATER PIXIES AND CHAOTICALLY ALIGNED
BARDS IN OKLAHOMA

I saw the wreck bow to a choir.
That is a bird

I would not catch.
To give a mouthful of sunshine.

I have put off my coat how
shall I put it on?

Some kind of alternative mathematics
camouflaged between seven and eight.

A primeval laurel
leans to embrace
the household gods

with shade,
sixteen dark blue branches
a penny.

Yet a little sleep
a little slumber
a little folding of the hands

to sleep. It's not a man up there,
lo and behold,
a girlish tree in the moon.

THE LAKE BROTHELS OF THE NORTH

She comes out crying.

A little boy stares at her.

People start crowding around her.

Her soul seeps through the air, a row
of flame stretches down the road.

Thereafter the underside,
the bottoms of clues.

I bet you do.

The girl is got into her altitudes,
twinkling

upon my deluged eye,
the one who broke

the news to me.
Don't kill that half pint.

Torch-pregnant Dido
on book, as in water,

face answereth to face.
The one too luminous

on her ass.
A school for singing.

The stuff will be here
when the boat gets back.

She says I might get
loved if I could keep it hid.

Open thy mouth for the dumb in the cause
of all who are appointed to destruction,

she says. Weighing in at
106 lb, wet.

For she *is* his money.

BRICK RADIO

Everything is a *meer spunge*,
my business: interval, common

little patch
with the romantic name.

Hast thou entered into the treasures
of the snow, the treasures of the hail?

You start talking
like that, I might

ease you in.
Like almonds whose milk blurs

the smashed polygons of a glittering hide.

You ain't by yourself
neither.

It is the glory of God
to conceal a thing.

I like to peel it off
in long strips.

A prime example of penitential food.

I wouldn't even care I'd
do her and all seven of her personalities.

It has stricken me
—a Snow White phase—

and I was not sick.

They have beaten me
and I did not feel it.

They have closed the gate
to gods and fakers.

THE STILL DROWSY HARE

My chauffeur
and my bodyguard were trading puns

like a couple of zombies.
And for a second

I forgot that doors have door handles
and walls exist for a reason.

Tiger stirred a mill of noon prayers.

The way you got of doing
sugar better stop that.

Because I have called
and you refused.

I ain't gonna tell nobody
the way you do.

ANNIVERSARY

AMBIENT ASHTRAY

The fruit, a delicacy of autumn,
may be eaten *as is.*

In hock to what I see
of her mind.

Tit *tat toe*
my first go,

three little butcher boys
all in a row.

And we are locked in.

Obscure poets become expert
at cadging invitations and green

figs from a twice-bearing tree.
Reflecting fools.

My turn.

Don't leave the house.
Do what I tell you to.

The bells should filter all signals from the outside.

Indoor insolents.

She would spit upon her thumbs
and spread her own with it

that she might keep it all her to herself.
Hello someday.

At least we managed
a little pink in the outfit.

LIKE SHOOTING A DEAD HORSE THAT IS
CRYING AND TALKING

Nothing is lost,
they say,

and she reappears one day
out of the forest of the Western Highland.

Her eyes seem to make conversation
with the things they see.

Each afternoon lays bare
the rationale.

The crowd on the airfield begins to move
strangely, the whole thing stops

making sense
because she has lost sight

of anyone who knows her
and she hears nothing

of the jets twirling overhead,
only the billowy sound of her own name.

DAYS OF WET ORION

The party starts in one hour.
Look for me under the tulip tree.

A little ship needs but a little sail.

Yellowish vertigo,
spout of angels,

raw rum
and sudden noons.

With directions worthy of a cook.
I knew by that

way we got of losing
everything.

We could barely stand
the night's glare.

To carry two faces
under one hood.

Beggars would ride.

Children to bed
and the goose to the fire!

I knew.
Someone was putting her up

and buying her clothes and stuff. I met her twin
on the corner—you know about that.

SHUFFLE

When I go please
don't talk after me.

And the fluted blowing
of the mother-of-pearl

inlaid boxes
enlarged by the dark.

I tried to be oh tried
to be tried to be!

The dashboard alone
scares me.

So what if I give you my present
a little early.

ASTROTURF

Her favorite advice:
be Brechtian.
With earrings & adjectives.

While buttered larks
fall from the sky.
There's just no way.

Standing against a tin wall,
bird nailed to a mirror,
her mouth is painted with branches.

Discover not a secret
to another,
the good book says.

One small sip is quite enough
to make you think
you have entered another world.

And all doubt about which one
it is disappears at once.

She—yeah, Dido—starts hitting the guy
with her cigarette case.

And their sleep is taken away.

The green alchemy gives them
no peace.

I can't begin to explain
the world they left behind.

Or where that hunky Polo guy
trying to put out the flames with his shirt

came from.
I know I've seen him somewhere.

AND SHE WON'T COME OUT

crazy shoeshine boys

poivre à trois
the one who's late

glass globe
circled by a model plane

I'm going in
to bring my jane

home Nehi dresses
the idle brain

cellophane and wire
over the bone

a little bird came to bathe

NEMESIS

SHIRLEY TEMPLE WALKS OUT OF THE MEN'S ROOM

The man is opaque,
the skein golden.

Every one of his gestures
no matter how
sudden or slight
reverberates in the global texture.

I woke up to him
eating cereal out of my viking helmet
with a shot glass. No idea
where he got the milk.

But for the leprosy of things
I could see the river
a long way off, my silver
tenement through the reeds.

The only brook still babbling
after my sixth attempt at youth.

A plus and a minus
at the same time.

Whether it be bare
within or without.

Little drummer boy
eating everything in sight.

LOST LINER

On the wall is an Albers;
things twinkle in the lounge.

His angels be charged with folly—
it cracks between their teeth.

A boy rings a bell and the peeling
hatch opens again by itself.

Some fifty people are present;
most have a second helping.

Then, too, then, too, then, too.

Head bumper
Eyebrow branky
Nose anky.

Mouth eater
Chin chopper
Gully, gully, gully.

Tell you something
you might not like to know.

Milk is a popular soothing drink for children at bedtime.

More daring still are the birds.

Off to the terraces again,
without fault, without object,

steered by the waves, by coal dusts,
by fistfuls of red petals scattered to the air.

EXTINCT

You're gonna do what I say.

It will always be like this.

Hunter bent with the unwanted
gifts of hunting.

They keep you in a sanctuary.

DUTCH WOOD BEGGAR

           it says at the entrance.

You stop eating
and drinking until something

possesses you.
For the heart studies destruction.

I just came here to have
a word with you.

The room is white/ is charred/ is white.
The evening storm might blow.

Let go of the girl.

(Silence)

           Someone call the trainer.

Someone call the trainer.

DIORAMA

Why don't you come back tomorrow?

Or stay put. You could observe
a full minute of silence

before you start bawling.
You could visit that relic stand

of trees in the shade.
Either way.

The native women gather
lilies by wading into the water,
pushing a light canoe ahead,
finding the shoots with their toes
and tossing them into the canoe.

Something a little too "Lost"
about her spiel. Do mystery-cracked

ribs heal any quicker?
My cats marching around like zombies.

I wouldn't have fucked me either.

ONDINE

At the subway entrance
a frightened woman appears.

Behind the guide,
tinted by the Earth's

oblique veins,
a starlet appears.

People crowd into the Automat on the corner.

The flanking and flirting is that of many flags
at the gate of a monastery in flames.

Protected by a nebulous god
she crosses the street.

Hippity-hop,
fat and lean in 24 hours.

The waters hear the stones say
"Can't we all get along?"

A slight flush of red and one
looks into the scenario

as one gazes into an opal,
uncertain how far

the eye can penetrate.
We dig up a little dirt.

Tomorrow we shall eat
sandwiches cut into diamonds.

Flower.

LIFE JACKET

The thing is
those free hits
don't help.

"I'm Dido…I'm fine, but I need
my purse back. Please help me look for it.
I can't go home without it."

Not one false note.
At Pooh Corner
the secrets of her silver creed

take back ska,
the whole system of a breach
notwithstanding.

"Your landlord is awesome and your

clothes are on the roof!"
Hector flutters
and prances off.

KIDS WE CALL STARS

The day after the day
not yet called *unhappy*.

In a matchstick coach
on the ocean floor

burns the tiniest of lamps,
a liar's candle

painting the veil and her pillbox hat—
some pixie crying in a $500 outfit.

Now I never
will forget that floating bridge.

What the Japanese call
lost-roof technique.

Heart, liver, and lungs,
collectively known as the *pluck*.

Even a honey wagon.
They all disappeared.

What made me think
I could lock the pixie in her room?

Calm as a kitten,
she ripped through the door

and closed her eyes, asking
stuff about life on Earth.

SECRETS OF THE LATEST WINTER FASHIONS

Not daring to enter,
we passed near the little door.

Not daring to enter
the dark cells where all day

the mutants sleep
trussed up in gauze

and the latest machines.
The proud helpers do stoop under them.

What are you saying?

I saw a cottage near the sky.
I saw the Old World fixing lavender pie.

It's that simple:
you put your money

down, take your girl
upstairs and *clown*.

Neither shall your place
know you in the end.

Repeat.

I saw a girl just like a cat.
I saw a kitten wearing a hat.

I saw a man who saw these too
and said though strange all were true.

FRIENDS

FLESH AT WAR WITH ENIGMA

Moonlight will make you think
the streetcar is a toy.

Ask the elm tree for pears.

Burning for burning,
wound for wound,

stripe for stripe,
with every neptune fix

a tumbler creams another
sea horse, blossom-fret,

the blanche of blanchette.
Greetings destroy the heart.

And now I am their song—things
too rich for me.

I CAN EXPLAIN

He'll give them a slap on the buttocks
to calm them down.

The weakest go to the wall, I ask
no wild a-rushing.

And the sound of a shaken leaf
shall chase them

and they shall fall
when none pursueth.

It is not known how long
he was among them.

Not without binary residues,
barring functional-slash-animistic

criteria.
I knew he was the guide.

Skin man's hollering, passing
right by my door,

crying, "if I don't carry you,
carry somebody else."

SILVER TULSA

They had torn out the sink.

The fire technicians closed off the ramp.

We took advantage of the crowd
to hand out our boxes.

The sentries will pick up
the soiled shroud.

We made our way
to the railing too late.

Wow.

My friend faints at my feet.

I can't make out
the instructions,

the gibberish of the redoubling.
A guy dressed like a farmhand

orders a highball with lots of ice.
My friend is hurt.

A night to be followed
by a race between man and beast

to reach the legendary fruit first—
a child frightened by everything and nothing.

PALAIS JAMAIS

For the commandment is a lamp.

He wants to do me
James-and-the-Giant-Peach style.
Afraid to know what
that means but moderately excited.

Oh. The bar's closing.

A thousand English phrases
to learn by heart.

Little Bob Robin
Where do you live?
Up in yonder wood, sir,
On a hazel twig.

How to Use MetroCard.

Fifty for oral,
no touching.

TOM (TIMBERLAND)

dabble the wristband me
and the Timberland
I could swag my navy

blazer with a one-inch towel

to spat no more
but for why
I'm used to doing it

TOM (TUNNEL)

Because we can't take that autistic girl
we're babysitting on a blunt ride.

On tiptoe stealing chips and stuff.

Dear god you're not real thanks bye.

Surely in vain the net is spread
in the sight of any bird.

All the patio furniture
goes into the pool saying we

are building a castle.
Eyes empty, no,

the wrong side of town.
My friend wasn't home.

It's all coming back to me.

Dusty gowns,
unbuttoned boots.

We couldn't get her to the clinic
in time, her dad went crazy.

The sun came up.

Somebody scrawled on my door,
"The short drunk lives here."

People always coming over—
such a shy, *un*-shy girl.

A LITTLE HAZY ON THE DETAILS

I want it back.

I don't care if she bakes me a cake
with rainbow sprinkles in my honor.

Look out your back door.
Do you see Miss Chinatown

anywhere? I don't think you can
get a DUI on a living thing.

Just get him to swear
he meant to cough up the ring.

LIL WAYNE APPEARS ON A SWING

I send an angel.
I'm putting up with his SoBe Tea.

Beware of him
for my name is in him.

Sleepy man, my
mind keeps me sleeping.

In the secret places of the stairs.

Good-bye, sweet hat!

Wait.

Evening red and morning gray,
send the traveler on his way;
evening gray and morning red,
bring the rain upon his head.

The tender grass showeth itself.

So many days
I stoled away.

I don't care where I go.

TINK

If you don't want to talk,
    we won't talk,
I said. She set fire to the place.

I wonder what's the matter
    now, Tink
just broke her wand on me.

HIS NAME SHALL BE COVERED WITH DARKNESS

I saw it for the first time
only a moment ago:

a saucepan of Corinthian brass
made with such art

its contents cook instantly
and almost without fire.

A chafing dish of coals.

At least I got her to renounce her
washroom appts with Honey Boy.

She broke down.

The North Star shall guide you turn
left I'm the one wearing the prison hat

and holding one of those sugar-coated glasses
sailors use to make toasts to visitors:

Turn away thine eyes from me
for they have overcome me.

I'm going to sign your pitty
on the runny kine.

A frenzied flame
about the queen's bones.

I was angry with the world.

Black salt, flower of salt,
salt upon salt.

The watchmen going about the city
found me, to whom I said,

we have a little sister
and she hath no breasts;

what shall we do with our sister
when she must be spoken for?

The mandrakes give a smell.

Find me a dime,
Tiger mumbles.

I am afraid of all my sorrows.

ACKNOWLEDGMENTS

Some of these poems have appeared, often in somewhat different form, in the following magazines:

Boston Review
Conduit
Denver Quarterly
Fence
Intercapillary Space
Lana Turner
Poetry
Shadowtrain
The Offending Adam
The Volta
Verse

I want to express my gratitude to the editors of these journals for supporting my poems and for their efforts on behalf of the community of poets.

Special thanks to Peter Hughes and Oystercatcher Press for publishing the chapbook *Brick Radio* (Norfolk, UK, 2013), in which some of these poems appear.

Daniel Tiffany is the author of several previous books of poetry and literary criticism. In addition, he has published translations of texts by Sophocles, Georges Bataille, and the Italian poet Cesare Pavese. He lives in Los Angeles, where he is a professor of English and comparative literature at the University of Southern California. He has been awarded the Chicago Review Poetry Prize, a Whiting Fellowship, and the Berlin Prize by the American Academy.

Neptune Park
by Daniel Tiffany

Cover text set in Avenir LT Std.
Interior text set in Caecilia LT Std and Avenir LT Std.

Cover photograph © John Divola
From *Vandalism Series, 74V08, 1974*

Interior design by Cassandra Smith

Omnidawn Publishing
Richmond, California
2013

Rusty Morrison & Ken Keegan, Senior Editors & Publishers
Cassandra Smith, Poetry Editor & Book Designer
Gillian Hamel, Poetry Editor & OmniVerse Managing Editor
Sara Mumolo, Poetry Editor
Peter Burghardt, Poetry Editor & Book Designer
Turner Canty, Poetry Editor
Liza Flum, Poetry Editor & Social Media
Sharon Osmond, Poetry Editor & Bookstore Outreach
Juliana Paslay, Fiction Editor & Bookstore Outreach Manager
Gail Aronson, Fiction Editor
RJ Ingram, Social Media
Pepper Luboff, Feature Writer
Craig Santos Perez, Media Consultant